A PURPOSEFUL
REAL ESTATE INVESTOR

Copyright © 2021 by Tim S. Davis and Timothy D. Trimbath.
All rights reserved.

No part of this publication may be reproduced, stored in a retrieval system, or transmitted in any form or by any means, electronic, mechanical, photocopying, recording, scanning, or otherwise, without the prior written permission of the author.

ISBN: 979-8-7417011-0-2

Printed in the United States of America

A PURPOSEFUL REAL ESTATE INVESTOR

Using Real Estate to Diversify
Your Investments Without
Managing Tenants and Toilets

TIM S. DAVIS & TIMOTHY D. TRIMBATH

DEDICATION

We would like to dedicate this book to the hard-working staff we have been fortunate to have at All County® Polk and All County® Metro. Without them our systems and processes would not work, and we wouldn't be able to help the people we serve. We want to add value to the lives of the people we serve.

There are a couple of people on the staff who really need to be recognized. First is Shelbi Lankford. Shelbi is our bookkeeper and has been with us the longest of any staff member. Shelbi has really grown into a key person in the organization. Thank you, Shelbi, for all you do.

Second, we would like to recognize Jennifer Manning. Jennifer is our resident services coordinator. She is the liaison to the tenants and the potential tenants. She always has such a positive attitude even in a difficult situation. She communicates so well even when she has to deliver bad news to the tenants, they still respect her. Thank you, Jennifer.

There are many others who do such a fantastic job like Chris who answers the phone, Sandi who is our controller, Matt who coordinates maintenance, Derek who inspects the properties and all our vendors and contractors who help us to keep the properties in tip top condition. Thank you all. You are making the world a better place to live.

CONTENTS

Foreword 9
Introduction 11
Who Is A Purposeful Real Estate Investor? 13
Why Invest In Real Estate? 14

SECTION 1 | PURPOSEFUL REAL ESTATE INVESTORS

Purposeful Investor #1 – Gross Income of $250,000 • 21
Purposeful Investor #2 – From 60 to 600 Units • 23
Purposeful Investor #3 – Enough Cash Flow To Retire • 25
Purposeful Investor #4 – 100 Doors Before Retirement • 26
Purposeful Investor #5 – Cash Flow & Time Control • 28

SECTION 2 | BECOME A PURPOSEFUL REAL ESTATE INVESTOR

Process #1 - Acquisitions • 36
Process #2 – Rehab/Repair Properties • 48
Process #3 – Property Management • 57
Process #4 – Dispositions • 77
Putting It All Together • 89

SECTION 3 | A PURPOSEFUL LOCATION

Why Invest In Central Florida? • 93
Why Invest With All County®? • 98

About the Leaders and Authors 105
Acknowledgments 111
What Next? 113

FOREWORD

I first met Tim Davis at a real estate investors club meeting late in 2011. He was there representing his company All County® Polk Property Management. I was intrigued by what he was saying. It seemed to me he had a different way of looking at property management as his view was aligned with the mindset of an investor rather than just a Realtor®.

I was at the time looking at what I felt was the bottom of the market and I recognized this as a great time to buy real estate. I decided to give Tim a chance with one of my most recent purchases and I signed up with his company to let them help me with my properties.

They did very well, and I was pleased with the reporting and the care they gave my asset, so I started turning more of my properties over to them. As time went on, I realized there was a difference between what I had experienced with my other property managers and All County® Polk, so I eventually turned over all my properties in the Central Florida area to them.

As Tim grew his staff and sharpened his team, he added some people who really took his business to the next level. Tim Trimbath became the Director of Operations and things really began to take on a new twist. The team was really watching out for me as an investor even more than they did before.

The communication was great, and I felt like I was getting a great value.

Recently I relocated and decided to divest myself of all my Florida real estate. All County® Polk has helped me tremendously move through the process. They have been able to accurately value the properties and get top dollar for them negotiating on my behalf.

When I heard Tim Davis and Tim Trimbath were writing a book about what they have done for the investor community, I wanted to be a part of it. I just wanted to say I really appreciated all the hard work and effort they gave to make my investing in Florida a success. Good luck guys and God Bless.

Randy

INTRODUCTION

Most investors are struggling to maximize their return on investment. This book was written to help them use real estate to diversify their portfolio without managing tenants and toilets so they can maximize their returns and have full control of their time.

THIS BOOK IS NOT FOR YOU IF...

1. You are an investor who wants wholesale property.
2. You are an investor who wants to buy properties to fix-n-flip.
3. You are an investor who is looking for a "get rich quick" scheme.

THIS BOOK IS FOR YOU IF...

1. You currently invests in stocks, bonds or other volatile investments and you want to use real estate to diversify your portfolio.
2. You are a current real estate investor who wants to outsource the management of tenants and toilets so you can grow your portfolio without sacrificing time with your family.

3. You are a business owner, dentist, doctor, or professional who wants to build wealth using real estate without managing tenants and toilets. You want to become a purposeful real estate investor.

WHO IS A PURPOSEFUL REAL ESTATE INVESTOR?

A purposeful Real Estate Investor is a person who uses real estate as a vehicle to increase cash flow and wealth so they can ultimately have **control** over the greatest asset - **TIME**.

In this book, you will learn about some people who have started the journey to become purposeful real estate investors. Some of them have arrived at the ultimate destination and some are still on their way towards the ultimate destination.

We will share with you what the investors who has arrived the ultimate destination did. We will also share with you why some investors are still on the way towards the ultimate destination. You will learn from both types of purposeful investors so you can save some time, energy, and money.

In the meantime, let us proceed to look at the enormous benefits of investing in real estate.

WHY INVEST IN REAL ESTATE?

Benefits	Real Estate	Other Investments
1. Depreciation	This is a tax benefit that landlords receive from the IRS for providing housing	The US tax code allows for far more tax benefits when compared to other traditional investment vehicles (stocks, bonds, & mutual funds).
2. Cash Flow	Cash flow is a benefit that you can receive when there is money left each month after all expenses & debt service	Other investments might pay dividends but might not. Today, the gross yield of a typical investment property is 7%-10%. Compare that with the approximate 2.35% that you get with a 30-year US Treasury note, or even the 5-6% (give or take) that you can get from a no-load junk bond mutual fund.

Benefits	Real Estate	Other Investments
3. Lower Volatility	Real Estate far less volatile than individual stocks or stock indexes. The value does not usually move in either direction very quickly.	Individual stocks or even indexes can move dramatically up or down over the span of just a few days or weeks.
4. Inflation Protection	When you have a rental property, the tenant bears much of the inflations costs via the monthly rent.	While the S&P has outperformed the rate of inflation over the past 20 years, the investor has to bear those inflationary costs alone.
5. Investment Diversification	Real estate does not necessarily move with the stock market, so it is a good way to hedge against Wall Street losses.	A well-diversified portfolio can help you lower your overall market risk.

Let us explore each benefit in greater detail...

1. DEPRECIATION

Title 26 of the Internal Revenue Code Section 167 gives the landlord the right to depreciate property held for the production of income. I am not a CPA or a Tax Expert but from what I understand you can depreciate the building on your residential property over 27.5 years.

This allows you to offset income that you make from the rents and not have to pay taxes on it. This is a very powerful tool to keep more of the money that you earn as an investor.

2. CASH FLOW

Gross Rent - Expenses - Debt Service = Cash Flow. Cash Flow is what many investors are interested in receiving immediately. If you can accumulate enough Income Producing Real Estate, then the Cash Flow from the operations can replace or greatly enhance the income that you receive from your job.

Many investors start out with this goal in mind and over time realize the other benefits of Real Estate Investing, but positive cash flow is the icing on the cake.

3. LOWER VOLATILITY

While we have seen swings in the markets and there is sometimes no rhyme or reason why a stock might go up or go down one thing that we can always be sure of is that people need shelter. Because this is true and one of the fundamental needs of human beings Real Estate is much more stable as an investment.

It does not move up and down with someone's perception of what they think it might earn Real Estate Investing is a lot less volatile than other investments.

Take a look at the two graphs below from the Federal Reserve Bank of Saint Louis. Both start in January of 2015 and run through January of 2021. The first is the Dow Jones Industrial Average, and the second is the US National Home Price Index. Note that both move up and down, but not the erratic nature of the Dow as compared to the National Home Price Index:

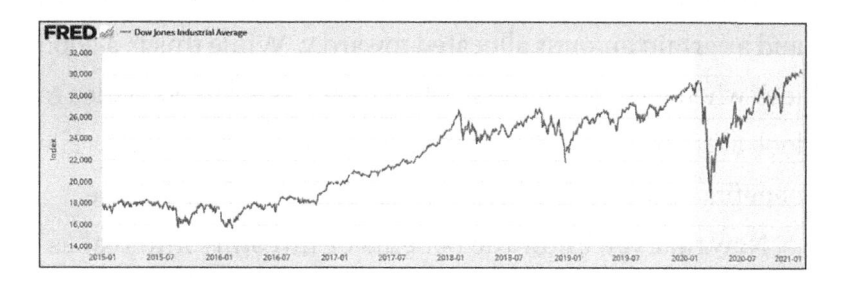

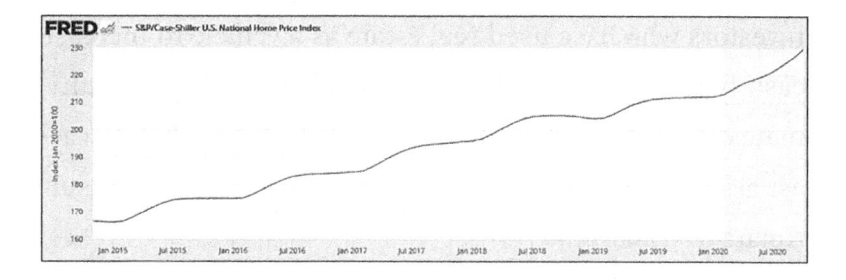

4. INFLATION PROTECTION

Inflation is inevitable in our economy. As time goes on everything seems to cost more. The average cost of a gallon of gas was $1.45 in 2000 compared to $2.45 in 2020. The average wage in 2000 was $42,148 and in 2020 it had increased to $49,764. As wages increase tenants are willing to pay more for rent.

The costs of goods and services increase as the cost of wages go up and it is a vicious cycle. The good news is that owning rental real estate protects you from the inevitable.

5. INVESTMENT DIVERSIFICATION

The term diversification has been thrown around a lot when being advised about investments. To have a balanced portfolio you need to have a certain amount allocated toward x and a certain amount allocated toward y. While this is a good idea when it comes to the stock market it is also a good idea to look at some hard assets in your portfolio like real estate. The benefits of diversification into real estate are listed above.

Now that you know the benefits of investing into real estate, let us proceed to read some stories about purposeful investors who have used real estate as a vehicle to increase cash flow and wealth. Some of them have arrived the ultimate destination where they have **control** over their greatest asset - **TIME**. Some are still on the way towards the ultimate destination.

01

PURPOSEFUL REAL ESTATE INVESTORS

may
jun
jul
aug
sep
jul
aug
sep
oct
125,058
125,487
124,000
105,450
86,502

PURPOSEFUL INVESTOR #1
GROSS INCOME OF $250,000

I met Diane in December of 2013. She was coming to Central Florida from a different country with some very inexpensive capital. She had a plan that I wasn't aware of when we first talked. In fact, after she told me what she was doing I thought it was a little crazy, but I was willing to help her to see her plan through.

She wanted to purchase 2 brand new homes and have them rented out for 5 years and then sell the properties. She already had the contract on the two properties she wanted to buy, and she hired our firm to take care of them as soon as they closed.

I looked at the purchase price of each of these properties. I calculated the potential rent and then looked at what the CAP rate was going to be. I came up with a number that didn't make sense to me until I understood the whole story.

When I did the math, I estimated that the CAP rate was only going to be about 5%. At that amount I was concerned that she would not be able to service the debt and make a profit. It wasn't until I found out about Diane's secret that the deal made sense.

Diane had secured 100% financing at a rate of .5% for 5 years. Yes, people in her country were more concerned about preservation of capital than they were interested in higher interests yields. The exchange rate was also favorable to the transaction at the time.

Diane used an LLC formed in the US to purchase the properties. Putting all the above factors together made up a sensible transaction. Diane was a purposeful investor and as it played out the properties were purchased in early 2014 and were sold in mid-2019.

We had collected $176,000 of rent for Diane during that time with those two properties and they also appreciated about 20% from the purchase price. When it was all said and done Diane had gross revenues of over $250,000 in those 5 years with basically no money out of her pocket.

This is not a typical story as you can't always make money like this, but it is an example of a purposeful investor. Diane had a plan, and I was glad to be a part of the team she put together to execute this plan.

You may not be able to get 100% financing at .5% from your lender but there is always a way to take the resources you have and create a unique plan you can use to build wealth.

Diane utilized our full services, so she was able to save time, energy, and money. Her properties generated cash flow for her while she had full control of her time.

PURPOSEFUL INVESTOR #2
FROM 60 TO 600 UNITS

Frank came to me in 2011 when he had just started a fund. He had gathered quite a bit of capital and had some of his own and was looking for a distressed property that he could buy, add value to it and then hold for a long period of time.

He would look at the on-line auctions, tax deed sales and foreclosures to find the property. Because he had access to cash, he could close quickly so he would bid on and buy anywhere from 5 to 10 properties per month.

Frank gave us the authority to hire a general contractor for him to get the properties market ready and then we would rent them out to start producing cash flow. Frank's plan was to assemble his desired portfolio in about 2 years.

Then stabilize the portfolio over another 2 years. After it was stable with some track record of steady cash flow, he got a portfolio lender to refinance the properties so he could get cash out to reinvest in more properties. This strategy is often referred to as BRRRR or Buy, Rehab, Rent, Refinance, and Repeat.

In no time at all we had built Frank's portfolio in Polk County to about 60 units. We stabilized them very quickly and were able to help him as many of the homes went through the refinancing program. Adding value through the rehab process, getting the properties rented at the top of the market and having a professional management team gave the lenders the confidence they needed to lend money to the portfolio knowing the assets were good solid assets. He was able to get great rates and 75% loan to value. Frank was able to satisfy the required distributions to his investors and made a very good profit for himself and his fund.

Several opportunities came Frank's way while he was doing this process and he was able to negotiate the purchase of a distressed fund that was going out of business.

Frank's portfolio got so large that he was able to hire full time employees to manage the properties in house. Last time I talked to Frank he had over 600 units throughout the state of Florida. It was a pleasure to help him get his start and watch him grow.

When Frank's properties were under our management at All County Polk, we helped him save time, energy, and money. Frank is a purposeful investor who now has consistent cash flow and total control over his most important asset – **time.**

PURPOSEFUL INVESTOR #3
ENOUGH CASH FLOW TO RETIRE

Tony wants to enjoy passive income for a long time. Tony started investing with us in 2012. He had very little money when he started but was able to find and negotiate some creative deals with the sellers. Not everyone can do this, but he seemed to have a knack to get it done. Tony's idea was to have at least some net positive cash flow at the end but not a lot. He was going to ride out the market for many years to come.

As rents rose higher and higher the cash flow would become more. As the properties would appreciate and debt was paid down there would be more equity that could be tapped in the future. Tony was very steady and thoughtful about his strategy. He would do all necessary repairs whenever we asked and kept the properties in good shape which gave him happier tenants that would stay long-term cutting down on the cost of turnover.

As prices rose Tony would sell off the less desirable units and set the money aside for opportunities that would come up. Whenever he was presented with a property that made sense for his portfolio, he would purchase it and continue the growth of units that he owned. Tony's long-term goal is more passive income. This strategy will work for him in the long run because rents are a good hedge against inflation so the income will rise as time goes on.

At this point Tony has a nice size portfolio and has very good positive cash flow. He could actually retire but last time I talked to him he told me he enjoys what he is doing. His plan is to have his passive income up to $20,000 per month through the real estate portfolio and his other investments. I enjoy helping Tony achieve his goals.

Tony has arrived at the ultimate destination where he has enough cash flow to retire, and he has total control of his most important asset – **time**.

PURPOSEFUL INVESTOR #4

100 DONORS BEFORE RETIREMENT

Monica is on a mission to have at least 100 doors before she reaches her retirement years. At this writing she is in her early 50s and told me she has about 15 years before she is ready to buy that sailboat and float around the Caribbean. Monica is very specific about what she wants to buy and does not get distracted by other things that might come her way. She is buying duplexes, triplexes and quads that are grouped together in bundled little communities.

Monica's strategy is to find units that are about 30 to 40 years old with some deferred maintenance. We help her get them under contract and negotiate a good price to allow for the improvements that she wants to make on the units. She then purchases the units with cash typically from a hard money lender partner who gives her the cash to purchase the units and money to fix them up.

After the purchase, the plan is to exit the current tenants if there are any. She then does a major renovation on the units replacing the kitchen cabinets with new cabinets and granite countertops. The interiors are totally redone with new floor coverings, updated bathrooms, windows, and doors. Most of the time the roof is also replaced and the yard nicely landscaped. She then has us market the properties at the market rent for those newly renovated properties. Typically, we are able to get 50% increases over the previous rent amounts.

When all the renovations are complete, and the tenants have been placed she then goes to a commercial lender and refinances the properties paying off the private money lender and getting a very favorable interest rate on the new loan.

This process usually takes from one to two years as she is typically buying from 8 to 18 doors at a time. At this time Monica has 38 doors and is well on her way to accomplishing her goal in the next few years.

Monica is a purposeful real estate investor who is on the journey towards the ultimate destination of desired monthly cash flow and control over her time.

Though she is till on her way, she is already saving time energy and money because she is not managing tenants and toilets. All County® Polk is managing the tenants and toilets for her.

PURPOSEFUL INVESTOR #5
CASH FLOW & TIME CONTROL

I was able to purchase my first rental property when I was 18 years old. It was an opportunity that presented itself and I took advantage of it. My father had purchased a rental property and then realized he didn't like being a landlord. He asked me if I wanted to buy it and I said yes. I quickly learned that I liked the idea of income from rental properties so I settled in and decided that I would study and learn more about it.

As I learned more, I was able to purchase more properties and actually worked my way up to buying commercial properties and renting them out to businesses. I did extremely well with my rental properties and made a lot of money however I was managing all of them myself.

In 2006 when everything was rocking and rolling, I decided to purchase a warehouse building and convert it to a shopping center. The property was on a major highway with a traffic count of over 40,000 cars per day.

I built it out and had an anchor store which was my business and 8 other retail units that would be available for rent. I was so excited as we had just finished this project about January 2007 and our business had just experienced the biggest year ever. Then everything came to a halt.

In November of 2007, I noticed that sales for our remodeling company were way down. I was not able to fill all my vacancies at the shopping center. My other tenants were having trouble paying their rent.

Things were changing in a big way. I was current with all my payments but was starting to run out of cash. Then it happened. In January of 2008, the bank shut down my line of credit and called the note due. I did not have the resources to pay the note off or keep our business alive, so I was forced into bankruptcy and foreclosure of the real estate. I ended up in December of 2008 bankrupt, broke, and homeless.

In 2009 I had to start from scratch. A friend of mine said "you have always been good at real estate; you should get a license". At that point I thought that might be a good idea because I needed to do something to be able to buy groceries. So that is what I did.

I started my real estate career as a buyer's agent with a big real estate firm and learned very early on that it was a hard way to make a living. As I started to ponder what I wanted to do and where I wanted to go in this new adventure the idea of a property management business came up.

I realized it was the perfect world for me. With my real estate and construction background I could really make this work, so I bought my first All County® Property Management Franchise.

We built our systems and put people in key positions as we grew the company. I realized early on we had built out processes and systems that were helping a lot of people earn passive income month after month. So about 2 years after we started the company, I decided it was time to become a customer of the business. I had owned rental property before but at that time I did everything myself. Now I had a team that was managing the properties, so I started adding units to my personal portfolio and allowed my well-trained team to manage them for me. This actually freed up my time so I could focus on growing my business and buy more properties for my portfolio.

I now enjoy passive income from my portfolio as I help other people do the same. I am very passionate about helping our clients create wealth through this vehicle. I am very thankful that I can do what I do. Every day is an adventure and I enjoy it so much that it never feels like work.

The first time I attempted to become a purposeful real estate investor, I failed miserably and ended up bankrupt, broke, and homeless. I had the wrong mindset which manifested in me managing tenants and toilets myself.

The second time I ventured into my journey as a purposeful real estate investor, I had the right mindset, so I handed over the management of tenants and toilets to All County® Polk Property Management. I am so glad I developed the right mindset.

I am passionate to help investors use real estate to diversify their portfolios without managing tenants and toilets so they can maximize their return, enjoy passive income, and have full control of their time.

In the next section, my co-author Timothy Trimbath and me will guide you through a proven framework or process you can use to become a purposeful real estate investor whether you are just starting your journey, or you have been on the journey for a while and desire to accelerate your progress towards the ultimate destination.

02

BECOME A PURPOSEFUL REAL ESTATE INVESTOR

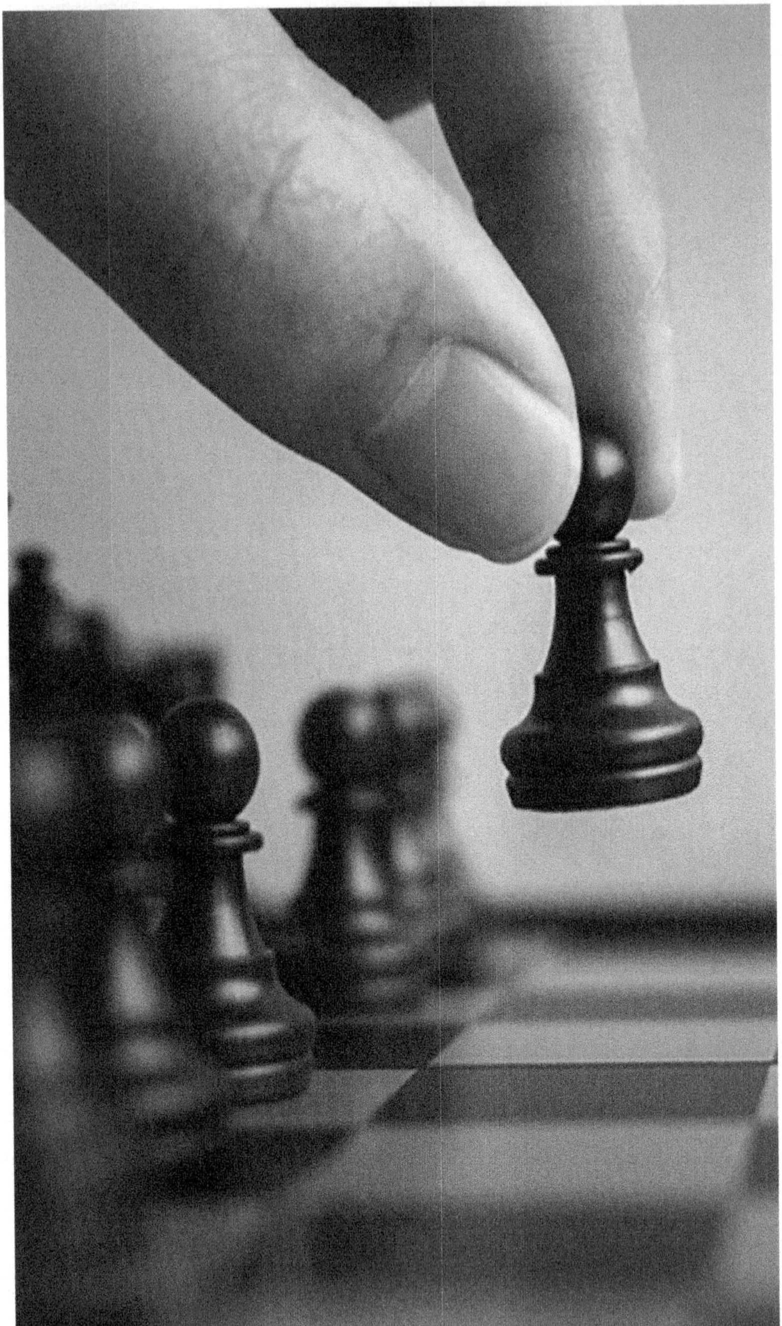

To become a purposeful real estate investor, you need a system. There are four major processes in a purposeful real estate investor's system.

Here is an overview of the four processes:
1. Acquisitions
2. Rehab or Repair
3. Property Management
4. Dispositions

Let us look at each process in greater detail:

PROCESS #1 | **ACQUISITIONS**

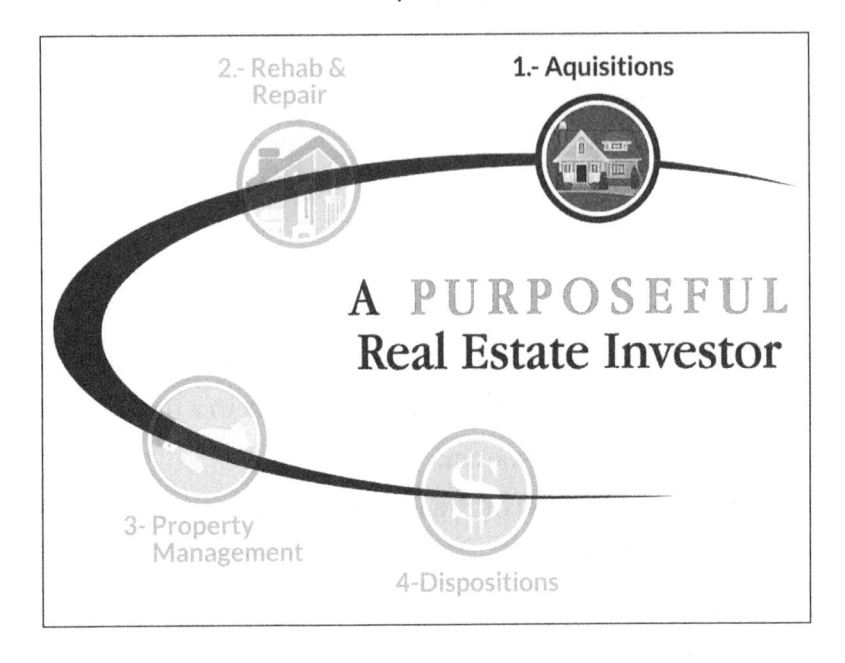

Diagram: A Purposeful Real Estate Investor — showing the cycle: 1.- Aquisitions, 2.- Rehab & Repair, 3- Property Management, 4-Dispositions

Three Types of Real Estate Investors.

There are several types of real estate investors. For the sake of simplicity, I am going to talk about only three in this book. When it comes to residential real estate the three types we usually see are; wholesaling contracts, fix-n-flipping projects and those who are buying and holding for the long haul.

All of these types of investments can be lucrative, but all are not created equally.

1. THE WHOLESALING INVESTOR

Wholesaling contracts is an area that a lot of investors like to start in. This doesn't take a lot of experience or cash to get started and you could get some quick cash. However, wholesaling is a job, and it does take some effort. Over time you could build a business doing this. A good rule of thumb to use for wholesaling is to get the property under contract at 65% or less of the after repaired value, minus the cost of repairs. This will give you some room to be able to sell it to an investor who would want to do the repairs and sell it on the retail market.

Some of the drawbacks are; if you don't get the property under contract at the right price you could end up falling out of contract without making any money. If you estimate the repairs wrong, you might get a bad reputation with potential end buyers. And last but not the least, this is like owning a job. All the income you receive from doing this is taxable at your regular tax rate.

I use wholesaling as one of my potential exit strategies whenever I look at investing in a property. It might be the best option for a property that I feel might not make a good flip or a long-term hold. The property might have more repairs needed than I am willing to do at the time. So, selling the contract to someone else would be the right thing to do in this situation.

2. THE FIX-N-FLIP INVESTOR

The second type of investor is the Fix-n-Flip Investor. This investor is one who finds and buys a property at a discount, repairs it to new or almost new condition and then sells it on the retail market.

As opposed to wholesaling, which can be done usually in 45 days or less, this process could take 3 to 6 months or maybe even a year depending on the complexity of the project. A good rule of thumb for this model is to get the property under contract at 70% of the after repaired value, minus the cost of repairs.

While the average profit on this type of deal can be $20,000 to $30,000, I have completed projects that paid $100,000 or more. There is however a lot of speculation in fix-n-flip. You are speculating what the after repaired value is going to be. You are speculating how much your repairs are going to be, and you are speculating there will be a good market to sell when you finish the project. It is possible if your calculations are off you could make very little or lose money for all your effort.

I had to write a check to get out of a deal on a project that I thought was a home run. There is a little more risk in this business model than in the former wholesaling model, but it can be more profitable and can become a business model with a great income stream. Keep in mind this is also considered a job and you will be taxed at your regular income tax bracket.

3. THE BUY AND HOLD INVESTOR

The third type of investor is the one we have been discussing throughout this book. The Buy and Hold Investor. This investor is in it for the long run. As the typical wholesale deal is done in less than 45 days and the average fix-n-flip is completed in 90 to 120 days, the buy and hold investor will keep his investment usually for 5 to 30 years or longer. This is definitely what we call the long game.

Buying at a deep discount is not always as critical in this model. You can make up for a premium paid over time, especially in higher-than-average appreciating markets. There have been several times I have purchased a property at the seller's asking price, negotiated favorable terms and created a win-win situation. The benefits you will receive from holding property long term are huge.

There are ratios and other indicators you can use to make sure that you are not grossly overpaying for property. Those indicators like cash-on-cash ratio, cap rate, gross yield and gross rent multiplier will definitely aid in deciding on what to buy and how much to pay for it.

Unlike the other two models discussed above, the income that you receive from buying and holding rental real estate is not taxed the same and you are allowed to depreciate the structures on the real estate which gives you a huge tax break.

Out of the three types of investors, the buy and hold model, in my opinion is by far the best for building long term wealth.

At All County® Polk, we only provide services for a purposeful real estate investor who wants to buy and hold for a long period of time.

Which Type of Property to Buy and Hold?

I have seen many people who have purchased property that was not suited for renting. A case in point was an investor who lived in New York City. This investor, because of their perspective, thought if they bought a bigger house, the house should be able to get more rent. At the time he purchased the property the average rent in Polk County was about $900.00 per month. He decided to buy a 6-bedroom 3 bath house in a rural community. He was confident the house was able to generate $3,500 or more for monthly rent because it was a big house.

He called me and was so proud of his purchase. He wanted All County® to manage it for him. He was surprised when we informed him the house probably couldn't get more than $1,500 to $1,700 per month for rent. I explained to him that at the time $3,500 per month rentals made up less than

1% of the rental market in Polk County. Even if we found someone who could pay $3,500 per month the chances of them wanting to rent this particular house were very slim.

We did place a tenant who ended up being a good long-term tenant but the highest rent we could get was $1,650.00. It was a learning lesson for him. He realized in order for him to maximize his return on investment, he needed to find properties appealing to a larger rental pool.

The mistake this investor made was to acquire his property without seeking counsel from a trusted professional who understands the rental market in the area.

A Win-Win Transaction

From time to time, we are able to list properties from some of the investors we work with who have decided to sell for one reason or another. Just recently one of those investors who moved out of state, decided to sell their Florida rental portfolio, and go in a different direction in his new state of residence.

As the tenants leases expired, we decided not to renew the tenants so we could we get the properties ready for sale.

Typically, we offer them to our other investors first if any of the properties is a good fit for them. If none of our investors is willing to purchase the property, we proceed to offer the properties on the MLS.

One of the properties we were selling made it to the MLS after about a week. Surprisingly one of our own Realtors was working with a new investor and they asked our Realtor® about it. We were able to facilitate both sides of the transaction and helped a new investor add his first property to his rental portfolio. The house now has a new landlord and both investors got what they wanted.

Both investors saved time, energy, and money.

Can We Acquire Properties For Investors?

Many of our investors want to be completely hands off. They task us with finding them properties with cash flow potential or rental properties already producing cash flow with a good return. We are often able to provide a turnkey solution for our investors. One such deal happened recently with a new investor from Virginia.

We had purchased a duplex from a family who inherited the property from their father's estate. It was currently being rented way under market and needed some repairs to get it to the point where it could be rented at current market rents.

We bought the property and began to make some of the repairs. We also non-renewed the current tenants so we could get higher rents and make the property more valuable. We finished the repairs and replaced the tenants within 7 months.

Once the property was performing well at market rent, we advertised it to our investor pool and through an off-market platform that is for investors only. The offer came in from the off-market platform and we sold the unit as a turnkey solution to a new investor. This investor was impressed with All County® and the way we operated so he retained All County® as property manager and has become a great new client who is allowing us to find more properties to add to his portfolio.

There are three ways an investor can acquire a property to hold for a long time:

1. The investor can acquire a property without the help of professionals like the investor from New York mentioned above. This approach can be costly and time consuming.

2. The investor can acquire a property or properties with the help of professionals like the investor who purchased his first property with the help of All County®. This approach eliminates costly mistakes and is less time consuming for the investor.

3. The investor can outsource the acquisition of a property or properties to property acquisition professionals like the investor who purchased a duplex with the help of All County®. This approach saves the investor time, energy, and money.

At All County® Polk and Metro, this is the process we follow when working with a purposeful real estate investor who wants us to acquire a property or properties for them so they can save time, energy, and money.

All County® Property Acquisition Process

This process has three steps:

1. CONSULTATION → **2. SEARCH** → **3. PURCHASE**

STEP 1: ALL COUNTY® CONSULTATION

- **Investment goals** – We find out what the investor wants to accomplish so we can determine the most efficient way to help the investor to maximize the return on investment. For many investors, the goal is retirement income, but each individual has their own reasons.
- **Buy Box** – We determine the most suitable property with the investor's investment goals. The property could be a single-family home, duplex, triplex etc.

We also identify the most suitable location to buy the property. We answer questions such as:

  ◦ How much will you spend to acquire the property?

- How much rehab are you willing to do? If rehab is involved, how does your all-in (purchase price + rehab costs) number need to compare with the ARV (After Repaired Value)? Example: Investor Ken buys an investment house for $120k, and he needs to spend $50k to get it market ready. His all-in cost is $170k. When the house is fully repaired, it would sell for $185k (this is the ARV).

- What is the minimum gross yield you want to see on the property? Gross yield = yearly rental income divided by all-in. Example: Investor Ken's new house is all rehabbed now and will rent for $1800/month. His gross yield is calculated as follows: (12 x $1800) / $170,000 = 12.70%

- What is your minimum cap rate? Cap rate is derived from the gross yield. It can also be expressed as your net operating income (NOI) / all-in cost. In Investor Ken's case, his gross income is $21,600 per year, and we can estimate that he will capture 60% of that income after he pays for management fees, maintenance costs, vacancy, etc. So, his NOI will be around $12,960 and his all-in costs were $170,000. This gives Investor Ken an estimated cap rate of 7.62%.

STEP 2: PROPERTY/SEARCH / DUE DILIGENCE

Once we know what you are looking for, we will then search the market in the areas you selected to find properties that meet your criteria. This is where our real estate analysis capabilities really shine! We will diligently analyze properties to find their true market values, rent price, and we can make an estimate of how much rehab is required.

If the property looks good on paper, we can help you write an offer for the property and get it under contract. Once you get it under contract, you will want to have a licensed inspector go through the home to make sure there are not any hidden problems that will cost you money down the line.

During the inspection period, we can also have a licensed general contractor look at the home to give estimates on the rehab required. We will compare these numbers to our rehab guestimate to see if the property is still viable for you. If everything checks out, we will proceed to closing.

STEP 3: PROPERTY PURCHASE

Your All County® Realtor® will work with the title company and your lender (if applicable), and you to shepherd the deal through closing. Closing is where the funds get transferred to the seller and ownership gets transferred to the buyer. If there are any bumps in the road, and there is always some problem that needs to be solved, they will work to take care of it with you and for you so that the deal closes, and you get your investment property.

We stay in constant communication with our clients so you can relax knowing your transaction is in good hands.

We have helped many investors to buy properties at favorable prices following the process above. We can help you too.

Go to **https://allcountyrents.com/appointment**

When you land on this page, select the area suitable with your current need and schedule an appointment with one of our professionals. We are passionate to help you achieve your investment goals so you can increase your wealth and have full control of your time.

PROCESS #2 | **REHAB / REPAIR PROPERTIES**

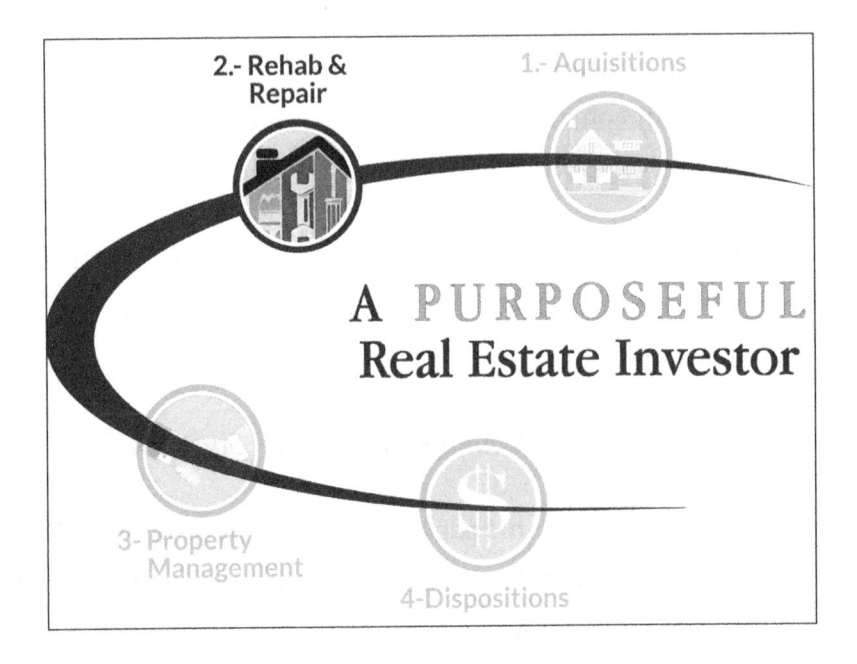

```
        2.- Rehab &           1.- Aquisitions
          Repair


                A  PURPOSEFUL
                Real Estate Investor


    3- Property
       Management
                          4-Dispositions
```

Before we begin let's define the difference between what a rehab is and what makes up just a repair. I have always separated the difference between rehab and repair by the dollar amounts that you might spend on something.

In most cases repairs come into play during a make ready of a rental property for the next tenant. I estimate that a repair on a property should be no more than 2 times what the monthly rent is.

Typically, in a situation like that the tenants deposit covers a lot of a repair. Repairs might consist of replacing a broken door or a window, replacing dripping faucets or screens, maybe some minor painting or touch up.

When it comes to a rehab typically this is done when a property is first purchased or after it has been in service for a long time. Rehabs usually consist of replacement of one or more of the 4 major systems, Roof, Electrical, Plumbing, or HVAC (air conditioning).

They could also be updating kitchens, bathrooms, and floor coverings. The cost of a rehab could be anywhere from $3,000 to more than $50,000 depending on what the complete scope of work is and what exit strategy the investor has for the property.

Many times, major rehabs are done on rental units when getting them ready for a retail sale to a homeowner to get the property in marketable condition.

Exit strategy can play a big role in the amount of money spent on rehab. If the exit strategy is to rent the property for a long term, then the investor may not do as much as they would if the exit strategy was to sell it on the retail market to a homeowner.

Tenants tend to be satisfied with practical features and lower rents than they would to pay more in rent and have granite countertops.

Whereas when getting a property ready for a retail sale the home buyer is looking for those really nice features in the house they want to buy as they will be staying there longer than the average tenant.

There are three major ways you can rehab or repair a property.

1. Do It Yourself.

Making repairs can sometimes be tricky. Many people do not understand the process or the licensing and permits that may be required to get things done. I was working with an investor just recently to purchase his property from him. He had gotten himself into some trouble with code enforcement.

The roof needed to be replaced and many of the windows and exterior doors were worn out. He thought it would be simple to just find some people that said they could do those repairs, buy the material from the local big box hardware store and his problem would be solved. However, after he did that his problems actually got bigger.

First the people that he hired did not install the roof or the windows and doors correctly. The roof did not have the proper flashing or underlayment. The roof was leaking worse than it was originally. The windows and doors were also not installed correctly and when the wind blew during rainwater would seep in around them and make a mess. And to top it all off the code enforcement agent happened to notice that there was being work done to the house without a permit.

The code enforcement agent slapped a violation on the home and gave the investor 90 days to make it right before the code enforcement board would have a hearing and impose a $100 per day fine for all the days that it was out of compliance.

This investor was beside himself. He called me to see if I could help him solve his problem or maybe even buy the house and take over the problem. These things can be corrected but to get them done correctly it might mean to actually redo everything that had been done with proper permits and proper installation. Knowing what to do and how to get things done is very important when dealing with residential dwelling units. After many years of experience at this we know and understand these things.

DO IT YOURSELF REHAB VS CONTRACTOR...

Verushka had a tenant who moved out of her old 1930's built house in Auburndale, FL. The house needed some rehab, but it was something that a contractor could handle in less than two weeks. Instead of using a licensed contractor, she had her neighbor do the work.

His work was very good, but he was slow. Two months went by and the house was still not ready. Verushka was taking it out on All County® that her house was not paying her any money while she had to pay electric, water, mortgage, insurance, etc. every month.

We gently reminded her that given the progress that had been made already, a licensed contractor could probably have the house ready in less than a week. She declined stating that she could not afford to pay anything extra.

Finally, about ten weeks after he started, the neighbor finished the house. We had the home professionally cleaned and it was back on the market for more money than her previous tenant had been paying. In less than three weeks, we found her an excellent tenant and the house once again started paying Verushka.

What Verushka failed to recognize was the opportunity cost of her money-saving neighbor's rehab. Our way would have gotten the property cash flowing in about five weeks. Her way took thirteen.

That eight-week (aka two months) difference cost her about $2000 in lost rent. Since the difference in what the contractor wanted compared to what she paid the neighbor was less than that, she would have been money ahead by hiring a professional.

A good investor never forgets that time is money, especially when we are talking about vacancy time.

2. Do It With Some Professional Help

Sometimes landlords have a handy man or a vendor that they have liked for years before they came to us at All

County®. That vendor might know the properties or have some kind of special warranty or deal that they have given the vendor.

We require that all vendors have proper licensing and insurance. When I am looking out for you and your property, I don't want to take a risk that someone who is unlicensed or uninsured does something wrong.

One of the investors that we work with had a guy like this. It was Dave the Handyman and Dave had been working on the properties for a long time and knew them inside out. The only problem that I had with Dave was that Dave refused to get liability insurance. Therefore, I couldn't hire Dave and pay Dave because it would go against our policy and I would be putting the investor at risk. However, I did allow the investor hire and pay for Dave when he wanted to use him, and we would use our vendors for everything else.

3. Hand It Over To A Professional

The most effective and easiest for an investor of course is to really be a passive investor. By that I mean there are only a few decisions the investor needs to make.

A great example of this is the story of Tony who was mentioned earlier. Tony has a long-term objective in mind. He allows All County® to manage the properties and really doesn't want to know every little thing.

He wants to be made aware when there is an expense over a certain dollar amount but usually authorizes most repairs without question because he knows we are looking out for his bottom line.

Tony analyzes his return on each property once per year and gets updated reports from us as to what the properties might be worth if we were to sell them for him.

If he has a property not performing to his criteria and the potential sale of that property would bring a better return, he gives us the go ahead to liquidate the property and look for another one that might bring the return for him that makes sense.

This is a process that continues to work for him and his portfolio.

When an investor decides to use the services of All County® to repair or rehab a property, this the process we follow to save the investor time, energy, and money.

All County® Property Turnaround Process

When you have a tenant move out, and you want to rent the property to a new tenant, the time in between residents is called "the turn." Having a systematic & efficient turn process helps keep your vacancy time to a minimum, and thus helps you make more money! Our process is below:

| 1. INSPECT | 2. MAKE RENT-READY | 3. LEASE |

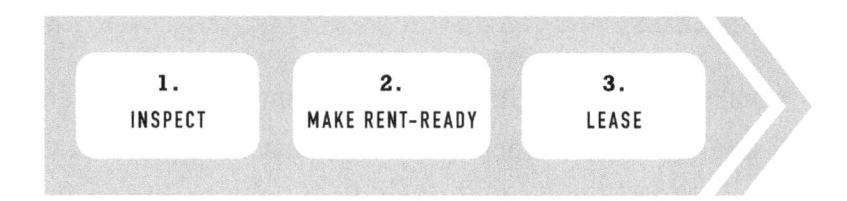

STEP 1: INSPECT.

Twenty-four to forty-eight hours after the old tenant moves out, we aim to have the property re-keyed and to have a detailed inspection completed for you. You will receive an instant alert that it is ready for your review.

At the same time, our RTM (Rehab, turns, and maintenance) coordinator will get the report and will begin making a punch list of things that need to be done to get the house rent-ready again. This punch list is called a "scope of work," or "scope" for short.

STEP 2: MAKE RENT-READY.

The scope includes the repairs that need to be done as well as the prices for each punch list item and the grand total for the project. We send this to you for approval, and once approved we dispatch a licensed contractor(s) to do the work.

The turn typically includes a standard cleaning, some number of little fix-it jobs, and carpet shampooing (if applicable).

STEP 3: LEASE

Once the work on the property is complete, we send an All County® RTM associate to verify that all repairs were made, and to take new marketing photos of the property. By this time, our analysts will have determined a new market rent price and submitted the price to you for your approval.

Next, we will utilize our extensive marketing programs to get your house in front of people looking to rent a home in our service area. As the rental applications come in, we screen the applicants on a litany of criteria including income, civil background, criminal background, rental history, and more. All County® will then place a well-qualified tenant into your home, and it will begin cash-flowing once again!

We have helped many investors to repair or rehab their properties and get them cash flowing quickly following the process above. We can help you too.

> Go to *https://allcountyrents.com/appointment*

When you land on this page, select the area suitable with your current need and schedule an appointment with one of our professionals. We are passionate to help you achieve your investment goals so you can increase your wealth and have full control of your time.

PROCESS #3 | **PROPERTY MANAGEMENT**

Three Types of Landlords

When you become a Buy and Hold Investor, you also get another label. That label is that of a Landlord. Becoming a landlord makes you responsible to care for a property that you get to rent out to a tenant. There are 3 types of landlords we will discuss here.

1. THE SELF-MANAGING LANDLORD

The first type is the Self-Managing Landlord. Many times, landlords self-manage their property for different reasons. Typically, the reason that they self-manage is financial. They feel like they can't afford to pay to have the property professionally managed. Therefore, they feel like they have to do it themselves. With this landlord there always seems to be a crisis that comes up. The mortgage is due and the tenant hasn't paid rent. The air conditioner has gone out and they can't afford to fix it and pay the mortgage this month even if the tenant paid rent. For this reason, there is no money available for a professional management company.

Others may self-manage because they want a job. They feel like they have to have something to do or have done it so long that they wouldn't know how to not do it. In either case managing tenants and toilets is definitely a job and if you choose to be a self-managing landlord then you should be prepared for the 2:00 am toilet overflowing or the occasional kitchen fire or non-paying tenant that has to be evicted.

This will be a constant job and depending on how many units you have you may find it hard to get away and take a vacation.

2. THE PARTIALLY MANAGING LANDLORD

The second type is the partially managing landlord. This landlord either likes to deal with the building maintenance and repairs or they like collecting the rent and dealing with the tenants personal drama but usually not both. If you are really handy and you like fixing stuff maybe you want to be the handyman.

You might want to be called out when the toilet backs up or the roof needs a leak fixed. Maybe you like hearing the story of why the tenant can't pay rent until next week or how their kids got a trampoline for Christmas and they want to put it in the backyard.

In this situation it may not be a full-time job but it is certainly taking your precious time to deal with these things. If you really like it and just can't live without it you can find professional management firms that might have a product that would give you some ability to do one or the other of these things. Getting help is just a phone call away.

3. THE PASSIVE LANDLORD

The third type of landlord is the one who looks at rental real estate as a passive investment. These are the ideal clients for All County®. These investors know that a good professional management team will add value to their investment. They will not suffer from decision fatigue as the only decisions they have to make is whether or not to approve a repair over a certain dollar amount.

This investor can spend their time doing things that they want to do. It might be working on a business venture, vacationing with their family or just enjoying free time wherever they are. The income keeps coming without their day-to-day involvement and they can enjoy all the benefits of long term buy and hold investing without the hassle of managing tenants and toilets.

Why Did I Do This?

I met a man who told me he used to be a landlord. He bought a brand-new home in Tampa and rented it to a lady. He chose to self-manage the property. John's idea of paradise was the Ozark Mountains. He and his wife regularly go on vacation there, and John has enough money to vacation for weeks & months at a time. After his tenant moved in, John's Ozark paradise became a living nightmare.

Picture John on the deck of a cabin somewhere relaxing. He's enjoying the mountain view, drink in one hand, book in the other, and then the phone rings. It's the tenant. He answers the phone, and she wants to report that the toilet lid is making a "creaking" sound when she moves it up and down. He suggests a quick spray with WD-40. She says that "maintenance is his responsibility." He sent a handyman over and went back to his book. The next day, she called reporting that the freezer didn't seem to be as cold as it should be. He asked if the food and ice were still frozen, and she said that it was. He told her about the dial inside the refrigerator that adjusts the temperature, and that she could turn it down.

She thanked him and hung up. This went on almost daily for the entire year that she lived there. Remember - she was the first person to EVER live there as it was brand new when she moved in.

John said that she seemed to look for things to call him about, and that his experience as a landlord was entirely negative. Had John hired a property manager, he would never have gotten those calls. At All County, almost every item he told me about would be categorized as "tenant responsibility." John could have enjoyed the Ozarks and the regular monthly income with none of the interruptions had we been on the case. In the end, he valued his free time more than the income and sold the property about a year after he bought it.

A *Peaceful Missionary and Investor...*

I want to share you Mary's story. She wanted to be an investor so bad. She would go to all the REIA Meetings and buy all the products from the gurus as they came through town. She had a goal of being a landlord to supplement her income because she wanted to be a missionary in another country.

She hired All County at first to help her with everything. Her properties were in disrepair so there was a lot of maintenance and repair that needed to be done.

Unfortunately, after a few months of these higher-than-normal repair bills she realized that the majority of the rent was going back to the properties and she was not getting to her goal.

Mary inquired about our lease only product and decided that she would take advantage of that and manage the properties and the repairs herself. So we were able to get all the properties occupied with tenants and turned everything over to her. Within the next few months several things went wrong for Mary. She used a friend to do some painting and some wood repair on her triplex. The friend fell off the ladder and had to be rushed to the emergency room. Since the friend was not insured, she felt obligated to pay for his medical bills hoping that he would not sue her.

She also hired an unlicensed person to replace a sewer line to another one of her houses. This individual got the yard dug up and began to replace the pipe. When the city code enforcement officer drove by and saw the unpermitted work going on he immediately shut the project down and sent a violation to Mary.

This caused delay and an upset tenant when they could not use their bathroom or kitchen sink for a couple of weeks while she worked on getting it resolved.

Mary worked through these problems as there were many more that she told me about. After about a year of fighting this frustration, she finally realized that it was taking too much of her time to do these things and that she would never get to her goal.

She decided to hand things over to All County® again and let us help her reach her goal. She finally made it to the mission field and her experience was much better knowing she didn't have to worry about her investments.

Trading Hours For Dollars

A friend of mine, we will call him Mike, had a corporate job making over $100,000 per year. He was very unhappy in his job because he really didn't like working for a big company. He had people that he had to answer to and was really tired at the end of each day and felt **unfulfilled.** Mike heard about passive income through real estate, and it intrigued him. He started going to the local real estate investors association meetings and reading books on real estate. It was very exciting as he saw a way to replace his income and maybe get out of his 9 to 5.

So, Mike started using the new skills that he had acquired and started buying rental real estate. As he added one and then another unit to his portfolio, he continued to reinvest all the money that he made to quickly pay off any debt that he had borrowed as he bought the properties. Mike would work the Land lording business at night and on weekends.

He was handy so he could do some of the repairs. The ones he didn't have the skills to do he would hire someone to do it and then he would supervise them to make sure it got done right.

He would also screen all his tenants. All the tenants had his cell phone number and whenever they would have a problem with one of the properties, they would call Mike. He would get calls all times of the day and sometimes late at night. It was starting to interfere with his performance at work, but he kept juggling it because he really wanted to leave his job and become a full-time landlord. Mike thought he was building passive income, but he didn't realize that he was really building another job to replace the job that he had.

It took Mike about 10 years, but he did it. He accumulated about 20 free and clear rental units and had gross income of about $20,000 per month from those units. After expenses (usually about 50%) Mike had a monthly income of about $10,000 per month. That replaced his $100,000 per year corporate job but he then realized that he had created a new job. And it seemed like many of the tenants that he had were very demanding because he had trained them to be that way.

I have talked with Mike several times and showed him how he could really live well and not have to do all that work but after doing it so long he is afraid to let it go and allow a professional to take care of things for him. Mike has a nice income. He can afford a nice lifestyle, but he is stuck in a job that he created and needs to break free to enjoy the time that he has. This scenario happens way too often and doesn't have to.

Time Freedom

> *"No man is free until he is free to spend his time the way he wants."*
>
> – UNKNOWN

My friend John on the other hand has a different perspective on his investing. John really likes his free time. He enjoys camping with his family on the weekends and during the week he oversees several businesses that he has created. John has put people in place in those businesses that run the day-to-day operations and he has invested his profits over the years in good solid income stocks and income producing real estate.

John looks at his investment portfolio as a business not a job. He has hired a professional wealth manager for his stock portfolio, and he has hired All County® as his wealth management team for his real estate portfolio. John doesn't know any of his tenants. They do not have John's cell phone. In fact, all of John's properties are owned by entities that keep his personal name anonymous from public record.

That is a little trick that we can help our clients with, so they won't be bothered with tenants or frivolous lawsuits.

John enjoys his time because he has a good team helping him. He is not doing any of the repairs himself. He does not screen the tenants. He has really created a passive income stream and is now enjoying the benefit of that. John started out learning about real estate the same way that Mike did. In fact Mike and John know each other. We all go to the same real estate investment association, but John took a different approach.

When a passive landlord decides to work with All County®, this is the process we follow to help the investor save time, energy, and money.

All County® Property Management Process

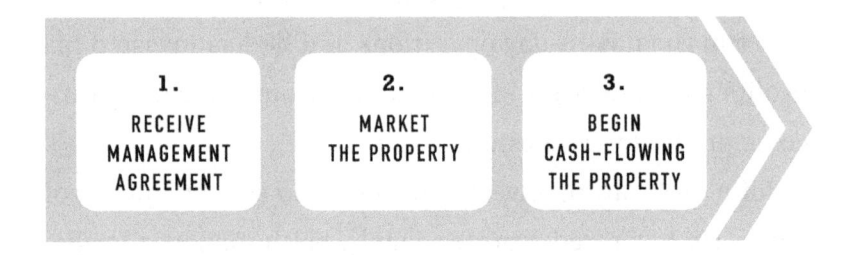

1. RECEIVE MANAGEMENT AGREEMENT	2. MARKET THE PROPERTY	3. BEGIN CASH-FLOWING THE PROPERTY

STEP 1: RECEIVE MANAGEMENT AGREEMENT

Once you receive your free rental price analysis and you have chosen the property management product that's right for you (lease only, flat-rate, full-service, or portfolio), all that remains is to sign your management agreement. We make it easy by pre-filling it for you and sending it to you for electronic signature.

STEP 2: MARKET THE PROPERTY

As soon as we get your signed management agreement, All County® Metro will get started on the business of finding you a quality tenant. We will have already helped you determine the optimal rent price, and you can relax while we do all of the work for you. We will advertise your rental listing on scores of websites including Zillow, Trulia, Hotpads.com, and many others. All of this exposure will result in pre-qualified prospective tenants visiting the property, which will result in paid applications. Paid applications mean serious prospective tenants.

STEP 3: BEGIN CASH-FLOWING THE PROPERTY

Just because a prospective tenant is serious about wanting to rent your home doesn't mean that they will be able to do so. All County® will screen all applicants on a stringent, but fair, litany of criteria including income, criminal background, civil background, and more. You can see all of the criteria by visiting *https://allcountymetro.com/available-rentals/rental-guidelines.*

After the tenants are screened and found to be suitable, we will set up a leasing appointment and place that tenant in your home. Now you have a qualified paying tenant and the rental unit begins to cash flow! Every month when your tenant pays rent, we will deposit the money into your All County® escrow account.

On or about the 10th of each month, we will send those funds to your bank account via ACH (Automated Clearing House) transfer. We will also put a detailed statement onto your owner portal so that you can see all of your income and expenses for the month, as well as a running year-to-date total for everything.

The ACH transfer can take up to three business days to get to your account, but we guarantee that if your tenant has paid their rent on time, your rental income deposit will be in your account and ready to use by no later than the 15th of any given month.

MANAGING TENANTS

Eviction Doesn't Always Mean Goodbye

Last year, we had a tenant named Shirly who stopped paying rent. We immediately sent out a 3-day as is our standard practice in case it goes to eviction, and then began making collection calls as per the US Fair Debt Collection Act.

The tenant informed us that she had lost her job and that she was seeking rental assistance. In the age of COVID, this was not an uncommon problem.

At first, the landlord was very patient with the tenant while we waited to hear more about her situation. We asked the tenant to send us copies of applications that she had sent to various government programs and charities to show that she was actively working on the problem.

Shirly didn't send us anything. Then she quit taking our calls or responding to our text messages.   Exasperated, we recommended eviction to the owner. The papers were filed, and Shirly was served notice shortly thereafter. That's when she finally called us.

It turns out that her daughter was very sick so Shirly took time away from work to take care of her. Instead of getting better under her mother's care, Shirly's daughter passed away, leaving her mother alone to face the tragedy of having to bury a child. It was during this time that she lost her job and wasn't doing much about applying for assistance. Realizing that she had to go on with her own life, Shirly found another job and was calling us to see what could be done about the eviction.

We worked with the tenant, the owner, the lawyers, and the court to work out a stipulation agreement. Under the terms of this agreement, Shirly made a payment plan that she could afford to get all caught up on the rent and pay for all of the owner's legal fees.

Today, Shirly has made good on all of her promises and is still living in her home. We were all especially happy that we did not have to add homelessness to her troubles while at the same time, we took care of our client's interests. This one worked out well for everyone.

Why Sam Switched Property Managers

Sam is a new client, and he had been unhappy with his property manager for a few years before he made the switch to our firm. His old manager never would hold his tenants to account for their actions. Here are a few examples:

In one case, he had received a code enforcement notice because a tenant had a boat on the property. Rather than serve a 7-day notice to cure, the manager did little about it and Sam started getting fines from the municipality. Instead of charging these fines to the tenant (after all, it was HIS boat parked there, not Sam's), the manager paid them out of Sam's account.

Another time a tenant kept clogging up the septic system with baby wipes. For those of you who are unfamiliar with septic systems, they are only meant to take human waste and a little toilet paper. If you put other things down there (like cooking grease, baby wipes, etcetera), they can back up into the home.

Now you have the stench of untreated sewage in your shower, tub, or toilet and need a plumber immediately. After the first plumbing visit to unclog the line, the tenant was warned about what could and could not be flushed down the toilet.

A few months went by, and you guessed it - another backup. So the plumber went back and fixed it again. Normally the cost would be added to the tenant's rent as she was the one who caused the issue. Instead, Sam paid for this service again, and the next time it happened. The manager was surprised when Sam did not want to renew this tenant's lease.

The final straw for Sam was when he drove by a property that he had just re-sodded with new St. Augustine grass. In addition to his brand new lawn, he also saw a new playground set on the property. Sam called the manager and told him that he did not want playground equipment on the new lawn as it would kill the grass. The manager replied, "that's why I told you not to put down St. Augustine in your yard." We won't quote Sam's reply directly, but it went something like this: "it's my #$%!! house and I'll put down whatever #$%!! grass I want. You're #$%!! fired!"

A good manager would never have let some of these things happen. In the case of the code enforcement issue, what should have happened is that the tenant should have immediately received a call informing them that parking the boat there was illegal and that the municipality was going to start issuing fines.

We would further inform him that if any fines did get issued, they would be added to his rent. We would tell him that we were going to come to the property the next day to issue a 7-day notice to cure, but if the boat was gone, we would simply take a photo for the code enforcement officer and the case would be dropped.

If necessary, we would issue the 7-day notice, and if the boat was still there on the eighth day, we would start eviction for non-compliance. As for the wipes in the septic line, we might have made the tenant pay for the first backup. We certainly would have charged for all the subsequent backups.

Lastly, our lease explicitly forbids adding trampolines, above ground pools, and playground equipment without prior written consent. Had the tenant not gotten permission, we would have called to ask that it be removed. We would visit the property a few days later, issue the 7-day notice, and deal with it from there. I cannot imagine telling a client that it's their fault that the grass would die because they should have chosen a heartier variety.

Moving Day - Who are You?

Our policies and best practices all serve a purpose, and sometimes those purposes become glaringly apparent. Take the case of the move-in that was almost a disaster but wasn't thanks to our execution of best practices.

The Perfect-Tenant family had outgrown their old house and had recently secured a job that let them move into the big house with the huge yard that they always wanted. They saw exactly what they were looking FOR RENT in our portfolio.

Mr. & Mrs. Perfect-Tenant applied for the home, were thoroughly screened & approved, and set a moving day. On moving day, we had all of the lease papers prepared and went out that morning to do our standard move-in inspection.

The standard move-in inspection is designed so that we make a photographic record of the exact condition of the home as close to the day someone moves in as possible. Every wall, floor, ceiling, window, window covering, appliance, bathroom fixture, inside, outside, and you name it is photographed. This inspection is often done no more than 48 hours before move-in, but is often done the same day so the tenant can't say that something "was like that when I moved in."

Getting back to the Perfect-Tenant family, we did the move-in inspection in the morning and they signed the lease and got keys in the early afternoon. Upon arriving at their new home, they noticed that a moving van was in front of the house and that another family was moving in! They called us immediately. We called the police and went straight to the house. The family that was moving in was Mr. Wegot-Scammed and his two boys.

The police were going to say that since Mr. Wegot-Scammed was already kind of moved in, we should go through eviction to remove them and the Perfect-Tenants would have to go somewhere else while it got sorted out. Then we showed the office the move-in inspection from a few hours earlier showing an empty house. We also pointed out that the locks had been changed (ours were lying on the floor in front of the garage door) by whoever scammed

Mr. Wegot-Scammed. He then asked Wegot-Scammed about how he came to be there.

It turns out that the Wegot-Scammed saw a phony ad for the house on Craig's List that morning. The phony ad said rent was about 60% of market rent and included all utilities! What a deal!!! In between the time that we inspected the house early that morning and about noontime, the scammer changed the locks on the house and installed a lockbox on the front door so that a potential victim could view the home.

Wegot-Scammed looked at the house and told the scammer he would take it. The scammer said that all he had to do was wire $1500 for security deposit and rent to some account, take the key out of the box, and DocuSign a phony lease. He could move in that very afternoon.

After hearing all of the stories and seeing our inspection report from a few hours earlier, the officer informed Mr. Wegot-Scammed that he was the victim of a fraud and would have to put his belongings back into the van and vacate the premises. A little while later, the Perfect-Tenant started unloading their van and are still living in the home today. Had we not had that inspection report, management agreement, and advertising all at the ready on our phone app, the story could have turned out very differently for the tenants and our client.

MANAGING TOILETS

The second most important aspect in property management is maintenance of the property. We call it *managing toilets*. The value of a property is preserved and increased through the careful management of the property.

Proactive routine maintenance is absolutely necessary to keep the property in top shape.

We have helped many investors to manage their tenants and toilets profitably following the property management process above. We can help you too.

> Go to *https://allcountyrents.com/appointment*

When you land on this page, select the area suitable with your current need and schedule an appointment with one of our professionals. We are passionate to help you achieve your investment goals so you can increase your wealth and have full control of your time.

PROCESS #4 | DISPOSITIONS

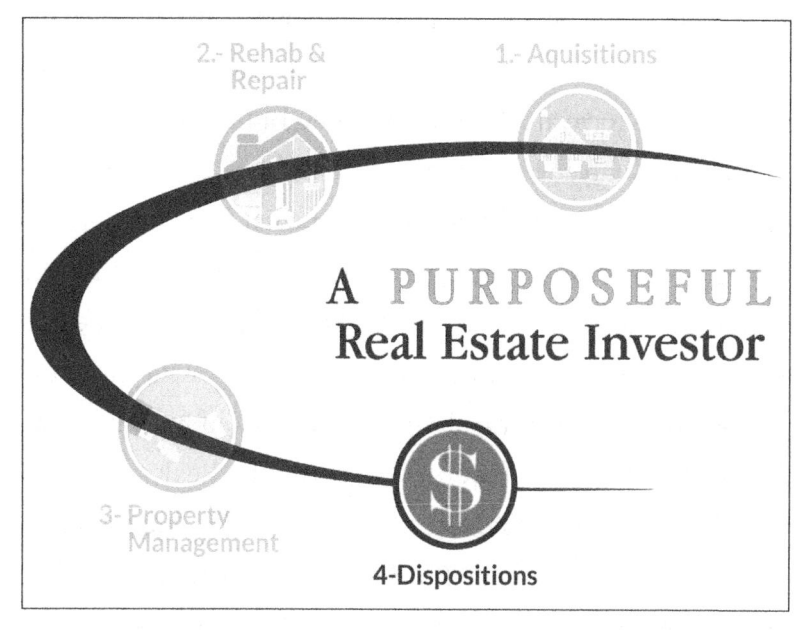

![Diagram showing A Purposeful Real Estate Investor cycle with 1-Acquisitions, 2-Rehab & Repair, 3-Property Management, and 4-Dispositions highlighted]

2.- Rehab & Repair
1.- Aquisitions

A PURPOSEFUL
Real Estate Investor

3- Property Management

4-Dispositions

In some ways, selling a property is just like selling any other asset, but it can be a little tricky. If you wanted to sell your car, you could consult the Kelley Blue Book® to see what it is worth. Selling a piece of jewelry? You could look at Ebay and other like websites to see how much similar items are selling for. Unlike mass-produced items, antiques, etc., no two houses are exactly alike. Even homes built by the same builder, in the same neighborhood, with the same floor plan will have some differences.

How do you price that? Once you pick a price, how do you go about letting people know it's for sale? Put a sign in your yard? Put flyers up around town? When people do show up to see the property, are they really qualified buyers? Once you come to an agreement, what do you do then? There's a lot to know, but that's where trained Realtors® like the ones we have at All County® come in handy.

We can analyze almost any property to give you an accurate market value and help you to market your property to buyers across town and across the country. Handling the negotiations, contracts, inspections, and getting the deal to closing is second nature to us. According to the National Association of Realtors, of all the houses sold in 2020 in the United States, just 8% were done without a Realtor®.

Why not do it alone? Read on to see what happened to some FSBO (pronounced FIZ-bo, and it stands for (For Sale By Owner) sellers who were sure they knew it all and didn't need any help.

'I overpriced my home and stuck around during showings.'

"I tried to sell my home FSBO, and it was a disaster. First, I was so eager to showcase my home that I hung around during showings, which was a huge turnoff to potential buyers. I thought I was being helpful, pointing out extra storage and other features, but looking back, I realize now that I was just an annoyance. And I overpriced the house, which is another common FSBO error. I wrongfully assumed that someone would make an offer anyway, and

that I need a strong starting point from which to negotiate down. But it just prevented buyers from even considering it. In hindsight, it would have been money well spent to work with an experienced agent."

– **MORGAN FRANKLIN**, LEXINGTON, KY[1]

It is very common for sellers to think their home is worth more than what it is. Sometimes they will point out how much money they have put into the home for things like double-pane argon windows, or a fancy water softener, etc. Other times they say that "this is the nicest yard on the block and people will pay for the manicured garden look." Whatever the reason, overpricing a home is a sure way to ensure that it WON'T sell. Get an accurate Comparative Market Analysis (CMA for short) by a competent Realtor®/real estate analyst.

A CMA will show you how much comparable houses in your neighborhood have sold for in the recent past. The analysis considers the location, age, size, construction, style, condition, and other factors for the subject property and comparable. At All County®, we do real estate analyses every day for both market rents and market values. When the time comes to sell your home in Central Florida, let us

---

[1] Ericson, Cathie. "For Sale by Owner' Horror Stories That Reveal All That Can Go Wrong." *Realtor.com,* 18 ct. 2017, www.realtor.com/advice/sell/fsbo-horror-stories/.

give you a free CMA so you can know what the property is truly worth.

Also, when selling a home, it is best to take a walk or go somewhere else when buyers are coming over. This will give them the opportunity to relax, look over the home with their agent, and speak freely without worrying about offending the homeowner with frank talk about what they do and do not like about the home. Giving them the space, they need will go a long way toward turning lookers into buyers.

> **'I got ripped off during my own open house.'**
>
> *"It's the classic tale: We were going FSBO to save money. My husband and kids were out for the morning so I could oversee our open house without distractions, greeting people at the front door and letting them tour the house themselves. A guy came in and disappeared for so long, I finally decided to check on him. I found him in the kitchen, rummaging around the cabinets. He mumbled something incomprehensible then bolted out the door. I also saw he'd opened every bathroom drawer and cabinet. That's when I realized he had no interest in my house but was searching for prescription medications—and sure enough, a bottle of painkillers for my husband's bad back were missing. I called a real estate agent I knew, and he told me this was a classic scam.*
>
> – **Dina Ochs**, Wilsonville, OR[2]

---

2 Ibid

FSBO sellers take a risk when they let strangers into their home. Like this person found out, some people view homes looking for things to steal. There have been cases where a "buyer" was really just a crook looking to case the house to see where the valuables were and possible entry points. By using a Realtor® to attract buyers, you can be sure that the people who enter your home are just there to see if they want to buy it.

> **'I got conned by a real estate investor.'**
>
> "When trying to sell my home myself, I was approached by a 'creative investor' with an offer to lease my house for five years. The buy-out price he named was well above market, and I would have cash flow of about $500 a month above my mortgage. Who wouldn't take that deal? But what I didn't realize by not reading the fine print was that he was able to sublet the property—which he did. I wasn't prepared for that, and I didn't like the feeling that I'd lost all control of my home for five years with all my equity tied up in it. Luckily, there was a clause in our contract stating the deal was off if his first payment to me was late, and that happened, so I was able to back out. But I've since learned that 'creative investor' can be a code word for trouble!"
>
> – **Jay Seier**, Fort Collins, CO[3]

---

3 Ibid

Slick-talking real estate investors are always looking to take advantage of a real estate novice. Whether it's grossly under-representing the value of the home or structuring a purchase in such a way that no savvy seller would accept, you always need to be alert. A good Realtor® can help you cut through the sales talk and really break down the deal in such a way that you can determine if it really is a good deal for you, or not.

How All County® Realtors® Can Help

At All County®, we are committed to help investors sell their properties at top dollar. Here are some investors we have helped in the past.

NADIA'S HOUSE (AKA HOW ALL COUNTY® HELPED OUR CLIENT'S WIDOW)

We received a call from a man who had recently purchased a house and wanted us to rent it out for him. He was in the process of renovating the home and would let us know when it was ready. A few weeks later, he called back to tell me that he and his young son (10-12 years old) had been working on the home and that it would be ready soon. Weeks went by and he was not returning my calls. I assumed that he had changed his mind about the house, and I left one final message asking him to call me when he was ready to move forward, and to let me know if we could help finish any projects he needed. I never heard from him again.

Instead, I heard from his wife, Nadia, who informed me that Alexi had passed away from cancer, and that she did not want to be a landlord. Real estate was Alexi's thing, and she just wanted to focus on raising her boy now that his father was gone. I visited the home and found that it was almost ready. It just needed to be cleaned and to have some minor painting done in the kitchen.

Nadia was very short on funds as Alexi had sunk a lot of savings into the home, so she had to get the property ready on a shoestring budget. To help her out, the listing agent and another employee spent a Saturday working at the property and got it ready for market. Nadia paid for a few gallons of paint and some paint brushes, but they donated their time.

Better still, we got the house under contract for full asking price in less than 10 days. When the house sold, Nadia received a wire for all that Alexi had put into the house plus many thousands more. She was so happy to have the house sold and we were thrilled to help a dying man's last investment pay off nicely for the family he left behind.

A Happy Investor On Closing Day…

Mike has been investing in Florida real estate for a very long time. Over the years, Mike has worked with several management companies, but he was never quite satisfied until he met Tim Davis and learned about how we were so much more than just a property management company.

Our full-service real estate investment management idea appealed to Mike, and he soon honored us with his business. He instantly saw a difference in our approach to those of our predecessors. Namely, we always keep his best interests in mind. This fiduciary approach manifests itself in many ways:

We don't place unqualified tenants in his houses just to get a quick leasing fee.

We hold his tenants financially responsible for maintenance requests when they caused the damage rather than just passing the costs to the client. It's easier not to get into an argument with the tenant and hope the owner doesn't ask questions, but we don't operate that way.

We analyze his rent prices accurately and negotiate rent increases (when market conditions warrant) with his tenants rather than just offering new leases at little-to-no increases just to get the renewal done.

Mike is now looking to divest all of his Florida real estate, and our analysts help him determine the highest and best use for each of his properties as the leases expire. Based on market value and rent price, is it best to sell the property tenant-occupied or vacant? We help him decide and sell the unit at top-dollar.

We have now managed and sold several properties for Mike. Most recently we sold a house in Lake Wales right along a major highway. Over the years, this property has been used for both residential and commercial ventures, including as a psychic's office. As an aside, the city closed the psychic down, which made us question these particular psychics acumen. After all, shouldn't they have seen that coming?

Mike had tried to sell the property before, but he wasn't successful. The listing agent for this sale determined that the highest and best use for this house was as a residential retail sale. This means we would sell a vacant house to a buyer who wants to live there. Our agent helped Mike get the property ready for sale, determined the optimal market price, and sold the house in a very reasonable amount of time.

Being on a major highway made this the hardest property in Mikes portfolio to sell, but All County® made short work of it, and Mike couldn't have been happier on closing day!

Here is the process we use to ensure our investors sell their properties at top dollar.

All County® Polk Property Selling Process

| 1. ANALYZE | 2. LIST | 3. NEGOTIATE | 4. CLOSE |

STEP 1: ANALYZE THE PROPERTY.

We will perform an accurate CMA (A comparative market analysis) is a tool that real estate agents use to estimate the value of a specific property by evaluating similar ones that have recently sold in the same area) on the property to determine the property's current market value. The All County® agent will then send a very detailed report to the seller and make an appointment to call them to discuss the results. If the agent and the seller can agree on a list price, we will then move on to step two - listing the home.

STEP 2: LIST THE PROPERTY.

Once the seller agrees to list the property with All County®, we immediately send out all of the proper forms and contracts to get the property onto the market. All County® will take professional photographs of the home, enter all of the pertinent data into the MLS, and get the property on the market. All County® pays to have your property featured on scores of websites including Zillow, Trulia, Realtor.com, and many more. We also cooperate with every other real estate broker in the area, so oftentimes our listings appear on their websites too! All of these efforts are designed to attract buyers and get you offers as soon as possible.

STEP 3: NEGOTIATE.

Once we get an offer that you mostly like, we can help you negotiate the deal so that both sides are happy to move forward. Now the property is under contract, but the negotiations don't stop here. The next step is that the buyer will have a home inspector look at the property to see if there are any repairs that need to be made. We will help you negotiate which repairs you will make, and help you negotiate with the contractors to get the best deal. After the property goes under contract and through the inspection period, it's off to closing!

STEP 4: CLOSING.

The home stretch! During this phase of the transaction, the title company will ask the buyer and the seller for a myriad of pieces of information. They will run a title search to confirm the property's rightful owner, and a lien search to look for unrecorded liens, in addition to code violations, special assessments, utility, and open or expired permits issues that are associated with residential or commercial real estate. If there are any issues with the title, code violation, open permit, etc. these will generally need to be taken care of before the property sells. If the buyer is getting a mortgage on the property, the lender will order an appraisal to ensure that the property value is appropriate for the loan. When everything is satisfactory, the buyer and the seller will sign papers, the seller gets paid (purchase price minus closing costs, selling costs, outstanding mortgage balance, etc.), and the buyer gets the house.

We have helped many investors to sell their properties at top dollar following the process above. We can help you too.

Go to **https://allcountyrents.com/appointment**

When you land on this page, select the area suitable with your current need and schedule an appointment with one of our professionals. We are passionate to help you achieve your investment goals so you can increase your wealth and have full control of your time.

PUTTING IT ALL TOGETHER

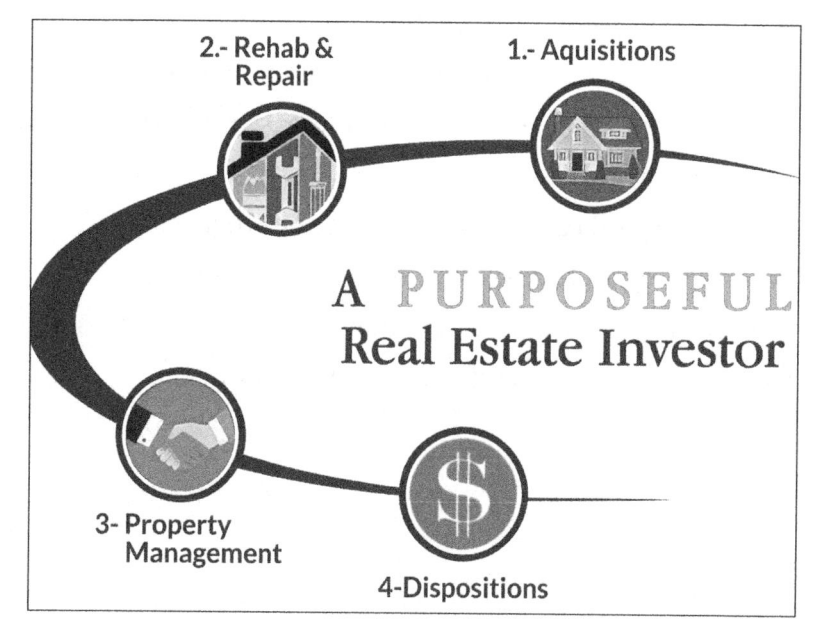

Diagram: A Purposeful Real Estate Investor — 1. Acquisitions, 2. Rehab & Repair, 3. Property Management, 4. Dispositions

A purposeful real estate investor needs a complete system to maximize return on investment.

At All County®, we have established a complete proven system which is made up of four major processes:

1. Acquisition
2. Repair or Rehab
3. Property Management
4. Dispositions

You don't need to reinvent the wheel. You can use our proven system to diversify your investments and maximize your returns. To start or continue your investment journey. Go to ***https://allcountyrents.com/appointment***

When you land on this page, select the area suitable with your current need and schedule an appointment with one of our professionals. We are passionate to help you achieve your investment goals so you can increase your wealth and have full control of your time.

A purposeful real estate investor needs to invest in a purposeful location to maximize return on investments.

In the next section, we will show you a unique purposeful location for a purposeful real estate investor.

03
A PURPOSEFUL LOCATION

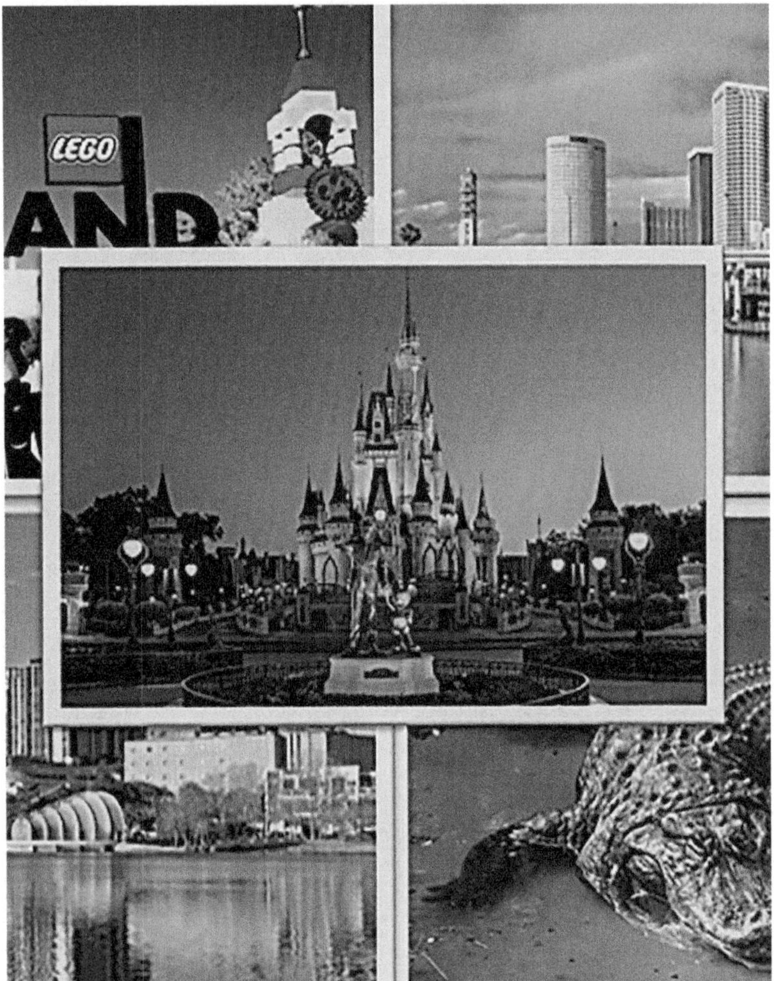
LEGO
AND

Why Invest In Central Florida?

A recent article in roofstock.com[4] identified several cities including Tampa and Orlando as some of the best cities to buy a rental property for investment in 2021. Last year was a particularly fantastic year for real estate in Central Florida. In Hillsborough, Polk, Osceola, and Orange counties, average single family home prices rose 12.5%, 10.2%, 7.8%, and 10% respectively.

After a great year like that, does it still make sense to invest in Central Florida real estate? Florida Realtors' latest housing report[5] discusses why they believe that the combination of low mortgage rates and high demand for Florida housing will produce keep the market strong for foreseeable future.

---

4 Rohde, Jeff. "Why Investors Still Love Florida's Real Estate Market in 2021." *Learn Real Estate Investing*, Roofstock, 9 Feb. 2021, learn.roofstock.com/blog/florida-real-estate-market.

5 "Sales Stay Strong - Really Strong - in January." *Florida Realtors*, www.floridarealtors.org/news-media/video-library/learning/sales-stay-strong-really-strong-january.

Here's why demand for housing in Florida in general (and Central Florida in particular) is so strong:

1. POPULATION GROWTH STATS

- Since 2010 the population of Florida has grown by 13.3% and is currently the third-largest state by population in the U.S.
- There are four Fl counties that are expected to add more than 1.6 million residents in the next ten years. Two of them, Hillsborough, and Orange, are in our service area. It is logical to surmise that the two counties in between Hillsborough and Orange will also experience strong population growth.
- Two of the four largest metro areas in Florida are Tampa-St. Petersburg-Clearwater with 3.1 million, Orlando-Kissimmee-Sanford with 2.5 million residents.

2. EMPLOYMENT STATS

- According to the Federal Reserve Bank of St Louis, the GDP of Florida has grown by nearly 52% over the past ten years to more than $1.1 trillion[6]

---

6 "Total Gross Domestic Product for Florida." *FRED*, 26 Mar. 2021, fred.stlouisfed.org/series/FLNGSP.

- The College of Business at the University of Central Florida (UCF) expects the Florida economy to outpace growth in the U.S. over the next four years.[7]
- Florida is home to 19 Fortune 500 companies including Publix Super Markets, & Darden Restaurants, which are in our Central Florida service area. Smaller company headquarters located in our area include Bloomin Brands, Badcock Home Furnishings, Marriott Vacations Worldwide, AAA, and Tupperware Brands.
- Florida has received numerous top rankings for its business-friendly climate: #2 best state for business, #3 corporate tax environment, #4 lowest private sector unionization rate, and is among the top five states with the best business tax climate.[8]

3. RENTAL STATS

- The vacancy rate among professionally managed, three-bedroom single-family homes for rent was 1.5 percent, with an average monthly rent of $1,455, up 11

---

7 "Florida & Metro Forecast: Robust State Economy to Remain Ahead of U.S. Outlook." *College of Business*, 2 Aug. 2018, business.ucf.edu/florida-metro-forecast-robust-state-economy-remain-ahead-u-s-outlook/.

8 "Grow Your Business in Florida: Enterprise Florida Inc." *Enterprise Florida*, 5 Apr. 2021, www.enterpriseflorida.com/florida-accolades/.

percent from a year earlier.[9]

- Only about 1 in 3 housing units in Florida are tenant-occupied, suggesting room for growth in the rental market.[10]
- According to the US Department of Housing & Urban Development, rents in the Lakeland-Winter Haven MSA have been increasing every quarter since 2016.[11]
- Rent Stats by Market.[12]
  - Rent = $1000-$2000/month
    - Orlando MSA: 80%
    - Tampa MSA: 70%
    - Lakeland MSA: 60%
  - Owner Occupied vs Tenant Occupied
    - Orlando MSA: 54% Owner vs. 45% Tenant
    - Tampa MSA: 55% Owner vs. 44% Tenant
    - Lakeland MSA: 59% Owner vs. 40% Tenant
    - Winter Haven MSA: 62% Owner vs 37% Tenant

---

9 Misztal , Maciej. *HUD PD&R Housing Market Profiles*. 1 June 2020, www.huduser.gov/portal/periodicals/USHMC/reg//LakelandWinterHavenFL-HMP-June20.pdf.

10 Rohde, Jeff. "Why Investors Still Love Florida's Real Estate Market in 2021." *Learn Real Estate Investing*, Roofstock, 9 Feb. 2021, learn.roofstock.com/blog/florida-real-estate-market.

11 Ibid

12 "Rent Easy, Rest Easy." *Apartments for Rent & Houses for Rent* | RENTCafé, www.rentcafe.com/.

4. QUALITY OF LIFE

- Florida is one of only seven states that does not have a personal income tax
- U.S. News & World Report ranks Florida as the 13th-best state in the country, including top ten ratings for education, economy, and fiscal stability.[13]
- Central Florida temperatures range in average from highs in the low 90's during the summer to average lows in the high 40's-low 50's in the winter.
- Wherever you go in Florida, you're never more than 60 miles from the beach. Sand beaches, a Florida signature, account for 1,100 miles (1,770 km) of the state's 1,800 miles (2,898 km) of coastline. Florida has more than 8,460 miles (13,620 km) of tidal shoreline, second only to Alaska in that category.[14]
- Central Florida is home to the NFL 2020 Super Bowl Champion Tampa Bay Buccaneers, NHL 2019-2020 Stanley Cup Champion Tampa Bay Lightning, MLB 2020 American League Champion Tampa Bay Rays,

---

13 "Where Florida Places in the U.S. News Best States Rankings." *U.S. News & World Report*, U.S. News & World Report, www.usnews.com/news/best-states/florida.

14 "Florida Fun Facts." *Florida Fun Facts | 2FLA Florida's Vacation and Travel Guide*, 2fla.com/florida-fun-facts.

and the soon-to-be NBA Champion NBA Orlando Magic*. Central Florida is also a big destination for MLB Spring Training. *Regarding the Magic, I don't know how many years there are in a "soon-to-be," but their time will come!

- Central Florida is home to some of the best theme parks in the world including Disney World, Universal Studios Orlando, and Legoland Florida.

Why Invest With All County®?

More than just property managers, we offer investors something unique in the Central Florida real estate marketplace - a full-service real estate investment management company. With All County®, you can make one call to handle all your real estate acquisition, management, or property sale needs. From wherever in the world, you are, we make it easy to buy, sell, and lease properties in the many different markets we serve across Central Florida!

1. YOUR BEST INTERESTS FIRST

All County® & Metro Property Management operate with a very different mindset than most property management companies. We do not look at ourselves as merely caretakers of your house. Instead, we operate with a financial services mindset, and while being a caretaker is part of our job, we recognize that there is much more to it.

Helping you maintain your investment portfolio is important, but we really focus on our duty to maximize your return and put your best interests first. We take our fiduciary responsibility to our clients very seriously, and this dedication to put clients' interests above our own manifests itself in many ways. Here are just a few examples:

2. REAL ESTATE ANALYSIS

We have some of the best real estate analysts in the business working here at All County® & All County® Metro. Want proof? Our senior analyst was a senior real estate analyst for Blackstone's Invitation Homes. That means that you get the same rent price and value opinions that a multi-billion-dollar corporation gets.

It would be cheaper to get a few realtors with 1-5 years of experience to give us value opinions, but then we wouldn't be offering the best to our clients. Whenever you buy, sell, or rent a property with All County® and/or Metro, you know you are getting the best possible price!

3. IN-HOUSE REHAB, TURNS, & MAINTENANCE (RTM) COORDINATION

We employ full-time workers to receive tenant work orders, dispatch them to contractors, inspect properties, and help schedule the services. We look at this as a cost of doing business, and we never markup maintenance invoices or charge a fee for handling these items for you.

We have heard of other firms that will charge a maintenance transaction fee or mark up each bill as much as 20% to offset their payroll costs. Still other firms will run everything through a general contractor, so they don't have to worry about finding vendors. This results in higher prices to the client because the general contractor marks up every invoice in exchange for overseeing the job.

Here at All County®, we deal directly with the contractors and make sure you are getting quality work at the best possible price. Keeping your expenses lower helps to maximize your bottom line!

4. SIMPLE TRANSPARENT PRICING

Some firms offer lower management fees for property management services to attract unsuspecting clients to their firm. While the property owner is looking at the "discount management fee," the company knows that their new client will walk through a minefield of miscellaneous fees. From set-up fees to vacancy fees, to maintenance charges, to inspection fees, after-hours call fees, and you name it fees. To us, this is a terrible way to do business.

Our property management services and charges are fixed and laid out on our website *(www.allcountypolk.com/pricing & www.allcountymetro.com/pricing)*. We have three honest fees, and that's all. This way, you know what you are paying long before you get your first statement. Helping you avoid unpleasant surprises when it comes to your money is just another way All County® puts your interests first!

5. EXCELLENT CLIENT COMMUNICATION

Whether you live down the block or on another continent, All County® & Metro make it easy to know what's happening with your property. Not only will you get timely phone calls, emails, or texts from our staff, but you will also get instant notifications from us too when certain events happen at your property. What kind of events trigger an instant alert? Here are a few:

- Online rent payment received.
- Move-in inspection ready on your portal.
- Move-out inspection ready on your portal.
- Annual inspection ready on your portal.
- Lease renewal finalized.
- Tenant maintenance request.

With All County it's easy to stay current with what's happening at your property. What's more, you will have your own web-based portal where you can review statements, inspection reports, and invoicing whenever it's convenient for you.

6. ACCURATE & EASY-TO-READ MONTHLY STATEMENTS

On or about the 10th of each month (in case the 10th is on a weekend or something like that) you will receive a notice that your statement is ready to view on your online portal. You will find a month-to-date total of all of your income, expenses, and net income for that month, plus running year-to-date totals. All of your income and expenses are categorized for you, any contractor invoices are scanned and easy to access, so keeping tabs on your investments & tax season can be a lot simpler for you!

7. NO HIDDEN FEES

With All County® Polk, you get a simple 3-step pricing structure, so there are no surprises!
1. Leasing fee
2. Management fee
3. Renewal fee

Hidden Fees	Others	All County
Set-up Fee	Yes	No
Maintenance Upcharge	Yes	No
Vacancy Fee	Yes	No
Annual Fees	Yes	No
Emergency Call Fee	Yes	No
Other Kinds of fee	Yes	No

Working with All County® saves you $200 - $500 a year from hidden fees. You also experience a peace of mind because no hidden fee will pop up to give you a heart attack.

In addition to the above reasons, All County® Polk and Metro have a dedicated and passionate team to serve you. The team is lead by Tim S. Davis and Timothy D. Trimbath – the authors of this book.

ABOUT THE LEADERS AND AUTHORS

All County® Polk & Metro is blessed to have two dynamic leaders who are the authors of this book.

Their passion, skillset, and commitment to help purposeful real estate investors to maximize the return on their investments cannot be rivaled.

Tim S. Davis' first investments were in business. He was an entrepreneur at a very young age. He calculated that a $50 lawn mower and a couple gallons of gas could more than pay for themselves the first day that you put them to work. When he was 12 years old he started his first business and did quite well as he earned over $3,500 mowing lawns that year. That was a lot of money for a 12-year-old. From that point on he realized that business was a good investment. You could invest a little into something that could produce future revenues. So, throughout his teenage years and into his 20's he was working on starting and working businesses. When he was 18 years old he was offered an opportunity to purchase his first residential rental property which he did. This further solidified his thoughts that investing in income producing assets was a smart thing to do.

Tim started his first full time business when he was 25 and invested all he had into the effort. It was a small remodeling company that started out small but within a few years he had added 8 employees and was producing well over $1,000,000 per year in revenues. He grew this company to the point where it was providing a very nice income and allowed him to diversify into purchasing rental income property. This was a natural progression as he had experience in this from the many different rental properties that he had over the years. Investing in business and real estate were the two buckets that Tim Davis used to build his net worth.

Over the years Tim Davis transitioned away from the construction and remodeling business to more real estate focused businesses. In 2008 after the big crash, he was having to reinvent himself. The remodeling business he had built over the 20 years prior had become a victim of the "Great Recession" and now he was starting over. He got his real estate license and began to help people work through the real estate market at that time.

In 2010 Tim came across an opportunity and decided to purchase the All-County Property Management Franchise for Polk County Florida. Because of his understanding of construction and rental real estate it was a natural for him to begin to help others build their portfolio of rental real estate.

He started with a few systems and a dream and within a few years had built one of the largest rental portfolios in Polk County. A few years later he got the opportunity to expand his market footprint in Central Florida and purchased the All-County Metro office.

Today with a great support team, headed by Tim Trimbath, Tim Davis is able to help many investors who invest in Central Florida become successful in their real estate investments. He really enjoys working with people to help them become a success.

Timothy D. Trimbath got interested in money and investing back when he was in high school. He gravitated toward the capital markets, learning all he could about common stock, preferred stock, investment grade bonds, treasuries, junk bonds, municipal revenue bonds, warrants, options, and almost everything else they trade on Wall Street. He earned a bachelor's degree in International Business from the University of South Florida and then went to work as an investment advisor representative (NASD 7 & 66) with a major Wall Street investment firm.

Tim earned an MBA in Business Management from Saint Leo University while he was working full-time for the investment firm. In the summer of 2005, he got the opportunity to take control of a startup retail company. Drexler-Witz, Inc. It was here that Tim met an individual who would change his view on investing forever.

The individual's name was Cody, and he was a very savvy real estate investor. The two became friends and used to argue amongst one another about who's preferred investment market was really "voodoo." Tim of course argued that stocks and bonds were the key to wealth, as the capital appreciation potential was so much better. Cody countered that when one owns stock, it's intangible and can drop in value in no-time flat for no apparent reason. Further, he argued, the dividend yields on stocks were laughable compared to real estate yields.

As time went by, Tim began to see that real estate investing was no more voodoo than any other kind of investing. He started to read about real estate investing and noticed parallels to Wall St investments such as yields, leverage, ROI, and more. In 2013, Cody was facing some challenges in the analyst room and asked Tim to come aboard as a real estate analyst. It was here that he really learned about buying investment properties, rehabbing them, and renting them out at top-dollar. Soon, Tim earned a promotion to Construction Resource Manager, and became one out of three people in the whole nation to oversee two regions (Tampa & Orlando).

Tim & Cody both left the real estate company and went on to another major hedge fund company. This one was a nationwide lending outfit that helped real estate investors gain financing. Cody was in charge, and Tim was the number-two manager helping to oversee lending operations in four states: Florida, Alabama, Mississippi, and Louisiana. Nothing in the hedge fund world lasts forever, and soon Tim began working as a Realtor® with Keller Williams.

Keller Williams taught Tim the mechanics of real estate transactions, and he used his excellent analytical skills to help retail and investor clients buy and sell properties. In 2017, Tim accepted the position as Director of Operations at Tim Davis' All County® Polk & Metro businesses. Today, he is pursuing his own real estate portfolio in order to grow his wealth and diversify his existing investments.

ACKNOWLEDGMENTS

Property Management for many years was a fractured industry. It was like the red headed stepchild of the real estate community. There were a lot of small mom and pop stores doing things so differently without rhyme or reason. Until a little over a decade ago when there popped up a few people who decided to put some organization to it and brand it.

Scott McPhearson and Sandy Ferrara were two of those people who had a dream to systemize property management. Their dream and concept led to the birth of All County® Franchise Corporation. I want to say thanks to them for their vision and for allowing us to be part of the organization.

All County® Polk Property Management was franchise number 7 of the over 50 franchises currently in the All County® franchise family. It has been a great journey so far and we are looking forward to many more successful years to come.

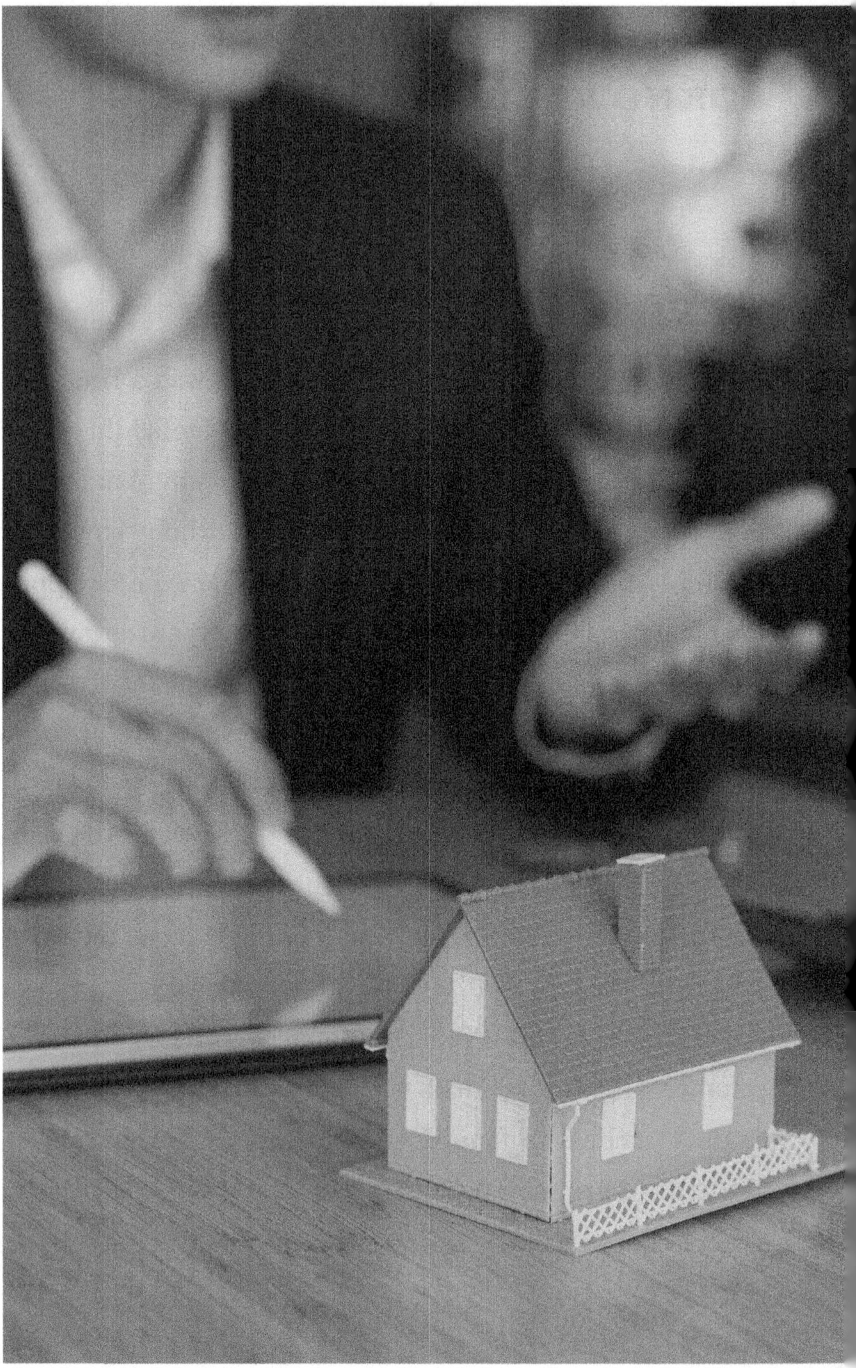

WHAT NEXT?

If you have not yet set an appointment to talk with a professional at All County® Polk and Metro, now is the time so you can start or continue your investment journey. Go to

https://allcountyrents.com/appointment

When you land on this page, select the area suitable with your current need and schedule an appointment with one of our professionals. We are passionate to help you achieve your investment goals so you can increase your wealth and have full control of your time.

OTHER BOOKS BY TIM S. DAVIS

THE 5 STEPS TO HOLISTIC WEALTH FOR REAL ESTATE INVESTORS

Order a copy at
www.yourhosticwealth.com/book

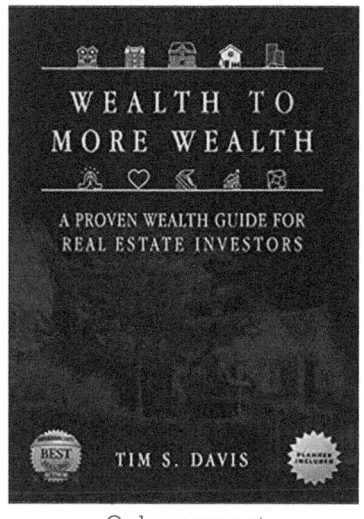

WEALTH TO MORE WEALTH
A PROVEN WEALTH GUIDE FOR REAL ESTATE INVESTORS

Order a copy at
www.yourholisticwealth.com/workbook

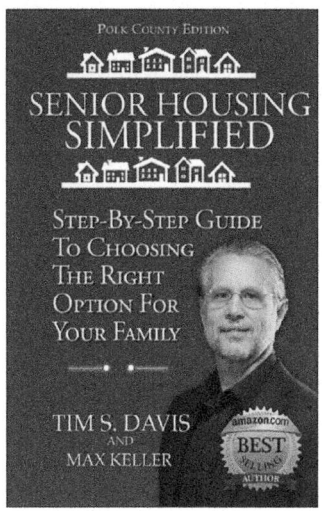

SENIOR HOUSING SIMPLIFIED
POLK COUNTY EDITION
Step-By-Step Guide To Choosing The Right Option For Your Family
TIM S. DAVIS AND MAX KELLER

Order a copy at
www.timseniorhousing.com

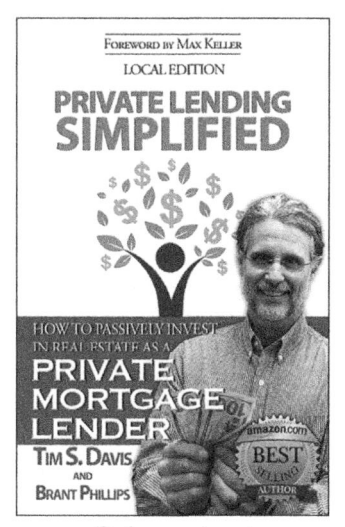

PRIVATE LENDING SIMPLIFIED
Foreword by Max Keller
LOCAL EDITION
HOW TO PASSIVELY INVEST IN REAL ESTATE AS A PRIVATE MORTGAGE LENDER
TIM S. DAVIS AND BRANT PHILLIPS

Order a copy at
www.timprivatelending.com